SAY **NO** TO

RACISM

Tips and Advice on
How to Be Anti-Racist

Rasha Barrage

summersdale

SAY NO TO RACISM

An Hachette UK Company
www.hachette.co.uk

Summersdale Publishers Ltd
Part of Octopus Publishing Group Limited
Carmelite House
50 Victoria Embankment
LONDON
EC4Y 0DZ
UK

www.summersdale.com

Printed and bound in Poland

ISBN: 978-1-78783-969-4

Substantial discounts on bulk quantities of Summersdale books are available to corporations, professional associations and other organizations. For details contact general enquiries: telephone: +44 (0) 1243 771107 or email: enquiries@summersdale.com.

CONTENTS

WHAT'S SO BAD ABOUT RACISM?   4

WHAT IS RACISM?   16

RACISM AND YOU   39

FIRST STEPS TO ANTI-RACISM   61

HOW TO BE AN ALLY   80

SUPPORTING AN
ANTI-RACIST SOCIETY   103

CONCLUSION   123

FURTHER RESOURCES   124

FOOTNOTES   126

WHAT'S SO BAD ABOUT RACISM?

INTRODUCTION

You, like countless others, have had enough of racism. The age-old problem has permeated societies worldwide, regardless of basic science, logic, reasoning, morality and plain common sense.

From wars, slavery and terrorism to street riots, police shootings and detention camps, racism's toxic and destructive consequences affect countless people around the world. In recent years, light has been shed on more insidious forms of racism, where racial bias and discrimination are unconsciously woven into the fabric of society.

The good news is that this situation is not inevitable: it does not have to be this way. You are lucky enough to be part of a unique turning point in history, where millions of people across the world are united in their sentiment: enough is enough.

History shows that silence has not been an effective tool for progress. Being non-racist while taking a passive and neutral position in your actions is not how change will come about. This book will show you how being non-racist does not equate to being *anti*-racist, and it will give you all the information and pointers you need to take the first step toward anti-racism – starting with some statistics over the next few pages to help you visualize the scale of the problem.

Anti-racism is a conscious effort to work against racism in all its myriad forms. An anti-racist person believes in racial equality, and applies that belief in their everyday conduct and decisions. They take action to challenge, deplore or dismantle the racism that they encounter.

For meaningful and permanent change to happen, your participation is needed. This book will help you to place your mark on the global change that is so desperately overdue. By expanding your understanding of what racism means, you can raise your voice against it and take charge of your own impact. Let's end the scourge of racism and create a different future.

THE ORIGINS OF RACISM

While scholars disagree about the exact origin of discrimination based on skin tone and heritage (largely because the definition of racism is not fixed), one thing is for certain: racism has been around for centuries.

Some trace it back to thirteenth-century England, when laws decreed the incarceration and expulsion of English Jews.

Others refer to the sixteenth century, when physical differences between Anglo-Saxons and Africans were used to claim a racial hierarchy that justified the slave trade at the time.

RACISM HASN'T BEEN AROUND FOREVER

Humans as you know them (Homo sapiens) have existed for around 200,000 years. Modern humans, meaning those that use tools and implements, have existed for around 12,000 years.

If we say racism is eight hundred years old at the most, that means it makes up less than 7 per cent of modern human history – or less than half of 1 per cent of total human history.

This shows that racism is not a permanent part of human nature. It is a temporary setback of human invention.

RACISM ISN'T BASED ON FACTS

THE TARGETS OF RACISM HAVE CHANGED OVER TIME.

IN SEVENTEENTH-CENTURY ENGLAND, IRISH PEOPLE WERE PORTRAYED AS "SAVAGES" WHO WERE INCAPABLE OF BEING "CIVILIZED".[1]

DURING THE LATE NINETEENTH AND EARLY TWENTIETH CENTURIES IN THE USA, THERE WAS WIDESPREAD PREJUDICE AGAINST ITALIAN IMMIGRANTS. THE LARGEST MASS LYNCHING (IN A SINGLE DAY) IN AMERICAN HISTORY WAS THAT OF 11 ITALIANS IN NEW ORLEANS IN 1891.[2]

THE MOVING TARGET DEMONSTRATES THAT RACISM IS BASED ON SELF-SERVING OPINION RATHER THAN ANY KIND OF FACT.

SEGREGATION IS MORE RECENT THAN YOU MIGHT THINK

There are people alive today who lived through the most unthinkable segregation. In 1960, six-year-old Ruby Bridges was the first Black student to attend an all-white school in Louisiana, USA, after passing the entrance exam. During her first year, federal marshals escorted Ruby to school due to the daily protests. She received threats of being poisoned and killed; one protestor held a black baby doll in a coffin. She was taught alone, as white parents refused to let their children be in the same class as a Black child. Her courage is seen by many to have paved the way for the end of segregation in schools.

| 1850 | 1900 | 1950 | 2000 |

THE OPPORTUNITY GAP

There is a persistent opportunity gap between people of different races around the world.

In Australia, in order to get as many job interviews as a white applicant (known as an Anglo), an Indigenous person must submit 35 per cent more applications, a Chinese person 68 per cent more and a Middle Eastern person 64 per cent more.[3]

In France, job applicants with Arab-sounding names get 25 per cent fewer responses than those with French-sounding names.[4]

LOCKED UP

The USA imprisons more of its Black population than South Africa did at the height of Apartheid.

One in three Black men in the USA are imprisoned during their lifetime,[5] with permanent consequences for their employability, housing and mental health.

This has wider implications for democracy and society; most states legally prohibit people with criminal records from voting. In the presidential election of 2020, 6 per cent of the Black voting population could not vote.[6]

STOP AND SEARCH

Police in several countries have been found to disproportionately stop and search Arab, Asian, Indigenous or Black people – a policy that has resulted in no significant change to crime rates.

In England and Wales, Black people are 40 times more likely to be stopped and searched than their white peers.[7]

Indigenous Australians are subjected to more strip searches: while comprising less than four percent of the New South Wales population, they represented 12 percent of all searches in a two-year period.[8]

RACISM IN HEALTHCARE

Racism exists in the healthcare systems
of many countries, leading to unequal
standards of access and treatment.

In one study, 29 per cent of white first-year
American medical students wrongly believed
that Black people's blood coagulates faster, and
21 per cent falsely assumed that Black people
have stronger immunity.[9] Such racist ideas lead
to inferior medical treatment for Black patients.
For instance, in the USA, Black babies are almost
twice as likely to survive if they are treated by
Black doctors rather than white doctors.[10]

Inaccurate beliefs can also be reinforced by racist
practices. Spirometers (that measure lung capacity)
in American hospitals often "correct" for race and
measure Black people differently – a policy that
is based on rationale dating back to slavery.[11]

DEATH IN THE TIME OF COVID

During the Covid-19 pandemic, Black, Asian and ethnic minorities were at a higher risk of in-hospital deaths caused by the virus in several countries, including the UK and the USA. Contributing factors included socio-economic status, geographic location, overcrowded housing and types of occupation.

In England and Wales — after accounting for age, measures of self-reported health and other socio-demographic characteristics — Black people were over four times more likely to die a Covid-19 related death than white people, while Bangladeshi and Pakistani men were almost twice as likely.[12]

15

WHAT IS
RACISM?

The first step to eliminating racism is understanding what racism is.

While you know that you want to challenge racism, you might be less certain about how to go about it. That is because defining racism is actually much more complicated than it first seems. What exactly *is* racism? How do you recognize it?

This chapter invites you to put aside what you think you know about racism and to open your mind to the myriad ways it can occur. By creating a clear definition of it in your mind, you will become more aware of its various forms and can work toward addressing it.

WHAT IS "RACE"?

The word "race" is around five hundred years old and was used originally in the English language as a marker of kinship or affiliation. It meant that you were a member of a particular household or group, or that you shared a common ancestor.

"Race" was redefined in the seventeenth century by white people to emphasize the perceived aesthetic differences between Anglo-Saxons and Africans, in order to validate the exploitation or domination over those they thought of as "inferior", and to justify the slave trade and colonization.

Today, it is a social marker of a person's identity, typically based on skin colour and other physical or biological attributes. Ethnicity is usually associated with learned aspects of identity, such as language, culture and religion.[13] As race and ethnicity are intimately related, this book addresses the ways in which both concepts are used to divide us.

WHAT IS RACISM?

Put simply, racism is treating someone differently on the basis of their race. It is usually evidenced by prejudice, discrimination or antagonism toward someone because of their skin tone or heritage, based on the belief that one's own race is superior.

It is founded on the (fabricated) idea that biology predisposes people to certain traits, abilities or qualities, determined by their racial group. It suggests that all members of a particular group are prone to certain behaviours and have the same level of skills (or lack thereof), which makes them inferior or superior to other races.

ARE YOU RACIST?

It is likely that you view yourself as a fair, open-minded person and you would baulk at the idea of being called a "racist". The term brings connotations of hate, anger and ignorance.

Nobody wants to call themselves a racist, because the word implies a fixed identity and motivation: a "bad" person to be shunned from mainstream society. This is misleading.

The word "racist" is better understood as a way to describe the *impact* of an action at any one time. It is less about what you think and how you behave, and more about the actions that make a particular race *feel* inferior or aware that they are *seen* as inferior.

WHAT CAUSES RACISM?

It is easy to think of racism as being caused by ignorant people who are filled with hate and bigotry, or that fear of difference is a natural part of human psychology that can extend itself to racism. But the fact is that no one is born racist. Racism is both scientifically and medically meaningless.

While fear, hate or bigotry may indeed be the cause of racist actions, it is the racism embedded in the structure of society that perpetuates the problem. The chain of causation always starts with the social structure and the systems in place, which *then* lead to fear, hate or bigotry.

DIFFERENT FORMS OF RACISM

Racism comes in many forms and plays a role in every aspect of life, from the way people interact with each other, to the ways we are educated and the stereotypes we encounter. Here are a few of the main forms you should know about.

- **Individual racism**: this refers to a person's (conscious or unconscious) racist assumptions, beliefs or behaviours. Structural racism (see page 23) provides a framework for individual racism to take place.
- **Interpersonal racism**: this means expressions of racism between individuals. It can be direct (such as using a racial slur or physical violence) or indirect/casual (also known as everyday racism, such as microaggressions). It usually follows a victim/perpetrator model.
- **Systemic racism**: this is about how society operates at large, rather than looking at one-on-one interactions. It is seen when policies and procedures result in the hierarchy of different racial groups. No individual racist intent is necessary for this to constitute racism.

Systemic racism shows itself in two ways:

1. **Institutional racism** – occurs within organizations. Examples include discriminatory treatments, unfair policies or biased practices that treat one race more favourably than other ones. Usually, racial groups are not explicitly defined.

2. **Structural racism** – the overarching system of racial bias in which public policies, institutional practices and cultural representations create or reinforce racial inequity. Structural racism is not created by a single individual; it is an all-pervasive framework and it influences every aspect of society. All other forms of racism emerge from structural racism. It is mainly characterized by white supremacy.

WHITE SUPREMACY

White supremacy is a racist ideology which supports the privilege, power, and preferential access and opportunities of white people over non-white people. It is founded on the belief that white people are the superior race and should therefore be in a position of dominance.

You may think that white supremacists make up a marginal portion of the population and that they have little tangible influence. There is, however, growing awareness that white supremacism as an ideology, rather than a political faction, is systematically entrenched within all aspects of society and we are all living under its influence.

WHEN IS RACISM A PROBLEM?

Racism is *always* a problem, for all members of society. Just as racism comes in many forms, so do its harms. The following is a list of some of the most destructive consequences of racism for those experiencing it directly:

- Hate crimes, including physical violence
- Police brutality
- Reduced education opportunities
- Reduced job prospects and scope for promotion
- Unfair treatment within the justice system
- Reduced chances of getting loans
- Impaired health and life expectancy
- Limited housing options

There is also growing evidence that links the experience of racism with mental illnesses, especially depression and post-traumatic stress.

DEHUMANIZATION

Dehumanization involves redefining the targets of racism, making them seem less human (or civilized) than other people and hence not worthy of humane treatment. Dehumanization is not limited to political issues. Any time someone is reduced to a single characteristic, whether positive or negative, they are being dehumanized.

Longstanding terms like "animals" and "vermin" have been used for centuries. They have been largely replaced today with labels such as "illegals", "parasites", "leeches", "rapefugees" and "migrants", referring to non-white people in non-human ways. All racial slurs are dehumanizing.

The impact of these terms being repeated cannot be overstated. In the five years leading up to the UK Brexit vote in 2016, the *Daily Express* newspaper had 179 front pages devoted to anti-migrant stories and the *Daily Mail* newspaper had published 122.[14]

HATE CRIMES

People from non-white racial groups are disproportionately victims of hate crime, which can take various forms, including physical violence and property damage.

The year 2019 was marked by the highest number of hate-motivated killings in the USA since the FBI started collecting this data in the 1990s, including the targeted shooting of 22 Mexican people at a supermarket in Texas.[15] In the year between April 2019 and March 2020, 72 per cent of all hate crimes in England and Wales had a racial dimension. During the Covid-19 pandemic, crimes against South and East Asian people increased after blame was put on China by some politicians and media outlets.

Hate crimes leave the individual victims, and the wider racial group in which they belong, feeling isolated and vulnerable to further attack.

POLICE BIAS AND BRUTALITY

The "Black Lives Matter" protests in 2020 were inspired by the devastating consequences of racism within police forces.

In the USA:

- A Black person is five times more likely than a white person to be stopped by police without just cause.[16]
- Black people make up 13.4 per cent of the population, but 22 per cent of fatal police shootings.[17]
- Among men of all races aged 25–29, police killings are the sixth leading cause of death, though Black men are two and a half times more likely to be killed than white men.

This double standard was clear when thousands of armed, (mostly) white, supporters of Donald Trump stormed the US capitol in January 2021, with minimal police action.[18] By contrast, unarmed "Black Lives Matter" protesters in 2020 were often met across the country with police in riot gear, military vehicles, tear-gas and batons.[19]

MICROAGGRESSIONS

Microaggressions are brief and commonplace displays in language, behaviour or the environment that make a person aware of being judged on the basis of their race. Some examples non-white people may have experienced are as follows:

- Someone crossing the road or clutching their belongings when they see a person of a particular race approaching
- Someone needing help in a public place but avoiding asking someone of a different race
- Someone mistaking a customer for a shop assistant in a store
- Someone mistaking a senior executive for a secretary
- Someone mistaking a lawyer for a defendant in court
- Someone mistaking a mother of a mixed-race child as the nanny
- Someone not asking for or listening to the opinion or ideas of someone of a different race

These experiences are common to the recipient. The offender may be ignorant of their effect and underestimate their impact.

THE IMPACT OF MICROAGGRESSIONS

Microaggressions happen all the time and it is easy to overlook their significance when taken as isolated incidents.

You may have asked or been asked questions, or made statements such as:

- "Where are you *really* from?"
- "You're so well spoken/articulate"
- "You don't look like a [name]"
- "I was not expecting that accent"
- "Tell me about your culture"
- "Can I touch your hair?"

While these statements may seem harmless, when heard over and over again, such apparently minor experiences can accumulate and leave a lasting impression on the recipient about how they are perceived in society, reinforcing the idea that they are different or do not belong.

THE BUILT ENVIRONMENT

Even the architecture and urban landscape around you can serve to further instil racism, in ways that are subtle but profound. For instance:

- Some bridges in the USA were designed to be low enough to ensure that buses could not pass under them, in order to prevent access by non-drivers, who would be predominantly Black.
- Walls, fences and roads have sometimes been designed to separate white neighbourhoods from others.
- In numerous cities, the wealthiest areas are difficult to visit via public transport. This keeps out poorer segments of the population, who are disproportionally made up of non-white racial groups.[20]

Architecture can be a form of racism that goes unchecked, because it seems wholly functional and its harm is not so immediately obvious.

MONUMENTS OF PAST RACISM

The year 2020 marked a turning point in the way many countries considered the portrayal of white supremacy, colonialism and slavery in their national memorials. In England, the statue of a seventeenth-century slave trader was dumped into Bristol Harbour and another outside the Museum of London was removed. In the USA, numerous statues were toppled, including several Confederate figures.

For decades, statues and monuments of men who played a pivotal role in some of the most savage acts of racism had stood proud and insulated from public scrutiny. But now, at last, because of these actions, universities and cities around the world are reassessing the symbolism in their monuments, as well as names given to buildings, and considering replacements that showcase justice, social repair and growth.

FAILURES IN EDUCATION

Alongside the scrutiny of monuments, 2020 was marked by increasing criticism over education syllabuses that minimize or entirely ignore non-white perspectives, innovation and history.

In the UK, students leave school with barely any knowledge of how slavery, the British Empire and colonialism have shaped the world. Likewise, history classes in the USA do not sufficiently address slavery[21] and Canadian education requires greater indigenous content.[22] The subject of racism itself is also not commonly taught, much less the notion of anti-racism.

Children have effectively been denied the knowledge that could immediately reduce the incidence of racism in their schools, as well as the tools to understand the wider problem of systemic racism in the world they will enter as adults. This failure is one of the reasons why racism persists.

THE PROBLEM WITH CHILDREN'S BOOKS

In 2014, articles in *The New York Times* regarding the "apartheid in children's literature" sparked a discussion and gradual shift toward greater diversity in children's books. Of 3,200 children's books published in the USA in 2013, only 93 were about Black people. This increased to 401 out of a total of 3,617 in 2018.

There is still a long way to go. An analysis of all children's books published in the UK between 2007 and 2017 showed that fewer than 2 per cent of their creators – authors and illustrators – were non-white.[23]

This under-representation creates a negative cycle that begins with non-white children not seeing themselves in books, and therefore not being "normalized" as part of society and not imagining themselves in inspiring positions. It deprives all children of the opportunity to understand other cultures and the value in human diversity.

TV AND FILM REPRESENTATION

The media plays a pivotal role in shaping your beliefs and perspectives about different racial groups. White people are over-represented and, at times, the only depiction for certain positive roles in society.

Many fictional shows and films fail to show Black or minority actors playing relatable characters with well-developed personal lives.[24] Criminality is mostly associated with non-white people, particularly Arabs in the case of terrorism.[25]

Studies show that your perception of issues is most heavily influenced by the images you see in the media if you have less real-world experience with the topic. This makes you prone to interpret media distortions and stereotypes as accurate representations.[26] For instance, you are more likely to believe depictions of Muslim characters as sympathetic to suicide bombers if you have no real-life experience with people who are Muslim, but you would be less inclined to believe the same portrayal applied to someone of your own racial group.

NEWS COVERAGE

Racial bias is a significant problem in mainstream news commentary. If we take mass shootings as an example, white perpetrators are typically "lone actors", but an entire race or religion is blamed if the shooter is Muslim. When a white man killed 51 Muslim people in New Zealand in 2019, some news articles described him as an "angelic boy" and "working-class madman".[27]

Likewise, in the USA, if white sports fans riot and cause criminal damage, words like "stupid" and "out of hand" are often used, while "thugs" and "lawlessness" are applied to Black protestors.[28]

Reporting also disproportionately focuses on crimes committed by non-white offenders. One study found that attacks by Muslim perpetrators receive 357 per cent more US press coverage than those committed by non-Muslims.[29]

This can inevitably lead people to perceive certain racial groups as dangerous and best avoided.

TECHNOLOGY AND SOCIAL MEDIA

It is easy to assume that technology companies are at the forefront of progressive thinking, and that technology itself is neutral to issues of racism. However, the way systems are built, how they're developed and how they're ultimately used can reflect the biases of the people creating them. Artificial intelligence requires training data and if that data is created by people who are biased, then the output will be too.

For instance, in 2020, an image-detection algorithm on Twitter was found to be cropping out Black faces in favour of white ones[30], and TikTok's content-filtering algorithm was recommending accounts of people who looked the same as the user (particularly in relation to skin colour and hair). Some everyday tools, such as soap dispensers and webcams, have been unable to detect darker skin tones.

INTERSECTIONALITY

Your identity is layered and multifaceted (comprising your gender, socio-economic background, age, etc.), which inevitably impacts your interaction with the world. Intersectionality is a way to understand how these various social identities can combine to create unique obstacles in life.

For instance, consider a woman who is Polish, Jewish and disabled. She may experience discrimination based on these identities collectively or individually, in different times and environments.

Racism cannot be considered without an awareness of other forms of discrimination that people experience. Each person's situation will be unique and shaped by all the different identities they carry.

RACISM
AND YOU

We all have an assigned racial identity that impacts our encounters with others and the way others relate to us. While this may not be a pleasant notion, your race is intimately connected to your life and will have had inevitable implications.

You may have been awarded certain privileges or disadvantages because of your race, whether or not you are conscious of it. Overlooking this means ignoring the racial hierarchies in society and the injustices that they create.

This chapter asks you to reflect on whether this social structure may have caused you to hold racist views, despite your best intentions and without your conscious awareness.

WHAT IS "NORMAL"?

The concept of whiteness is not a biological category but a constructed norm by which all "other" groups are compared.

This is explicit in forms that require you to select your ethnicity and "white" is the first choice. It is implicit in advertisements, the education system, Hollywood films, the news you read, and so on. For instance, books often only describe skin colour in relation to non-white characters, first-aid kits contain Band-Aids that only match lighter skin tones and news reports often use the word "community" only when referring to non-white people.

This normalization of whiteness accords benefits to those born within its definition; it is like an elite club that is paid for by the taxation of everyone else.

UNDERSTANDING WHITE PRIVILEGE

White privilege is the advantage you have if you are a white person in today's society; it is experienced regardless of anything you have personally done. It does not imply an easy life without other struggles or that any accomplishments are not deserved. What it refers to are the subtle benefits that a white person takes for granted every day.

It means:

- Learning white history at school
- Seeing white people widely represented on TV and in films
- Going shopping without security guard surveillance
- Not being questioned about your origin
- Succeeding without being considered a credit to your race
- Never being asked to speak for all white people

Recognizing this privilege can help you to understand the importance of championing anti-racist policies.

WITH PRIVILEGE COMES POWER

The flip side of white privilege is that it can be used to help others. It is not a burden to bear, but a way for the privileged to enact change.

If you acknowledge that you have white privilege, you can confront racial injustices even when it is uncomfortable to do so. By recognizing and understanding the economic and social benefits that come with being a white person, you can take action to change these norms in society.

Rather than feeling shame or guilt for inheriting a system that you played no part in creating, you can admit whether you have benefited from it and use that knowledge to promote racial equality.

BE COURAGEOUS

There is nothing pleasant about confronting potential privilege and racism within yourself. You need to be willing to identify your private and, at times, previously unacknowledged beliefs in order to reinvent your perspectives.

There is no need to put pressure on yourself to be perfect, to never say the wrong thing and to have a meticulous track record. Becoming anti-racist is about taking small and incremental steps to have a better understanding of who you are and what has shaped you.

The forthcoming pages invite you to find your courage to get out of your comfort zone and confront the discomfort. Only then can you make real change in yourself and the world around you.

TRIBAL INSTINCTS

While growing up around people who share your language, culture or skin colour may be comforting, it can also instil a heightened sense of suspicion toward people that appear different.

From a young age, your brain has been absorbing social cues about the racial hierarchy in society and characterizing groups into "us-versus-them" as a way to protect you from perceived threats.[31]

Think for a moment about your upbringing and how it may have influenced your mindset about racial diversity. For instance, consider:

- When you first became aware of your race
- Whether your family were all born and raised in the same country
- How you understood human diversity as a child
- Childhood interactions with people from different backgrounds or cultures
- How, if ever, you were taught about racial difference

You are likely to have an instinctive preference for certain races over others, without necessarily being aware of this bias.

ARE YOU BIASED?

Racial bias is a preference in favour of, or against, an individual or group due to their race.

These impulsive judgments are often rooted in inaccurate information and can be extremely harmful (such as in the case of police bias; see page 28).

- **Implicit** bias (or unconscious bias) refers to your internal judgments that occur outside of your conscious awareness and control.
- **Explicit** biases are judgments you are consciously aware of (for example, feeling threatened by another group and deliberately avoiding them).

Studies have uncovered overwhelming evidence that goals of equality and fairness are often undermined by implicit biases. It is a reality that affects everyone, including people who are themselves targets of racism and those committed to impartiality (such as judges and journalists). Every single person is biased to some degree.

WHY ARE YOU BIASED?

Your brain's need to simplify overwhelming stimuli means that it will take shortcuts, and quickly form associations and patterns in your encounters with people. The evolutionary reasons for this are understandable and these shortcuts are important to help you navigate everyday life, but this cognitive behaviour can all too easily result in lazy stereotypes and assumptions. These biases can affect your daily decisions and actions, including how you relate to people you deem to be different.

Children as young as three or four already look for patterns and are aware of what distinguishes them from others. The natural tendency of the brain to simplify and seek patterns continues throughout your life; it is heightened during times of stress (to avoid having to examine all of the relevant, surrounding information) and, most importantly, by social and cultural influences.

Your brain can only understand what it is shown, and that is why representation and dismantling stereotypes are so important.

WHAT SHAPES YOUR BIAS?

Influences from childhood, culture, TV, film, physical environment, advertising and social media can increase the implicit biases that you form. For instance, colourism (a bias toward lighter skin tones) has been shaped by: toy manufacturers producing figurines and dolls that are mostly white, the beauty industry marketing skin-lightening products, the fashion industry predominantly using white models, and the film industry generally casting actors with lighter skin tones in leading roles.

The way the media uses language can also ingrain specific biases in your mind.[32] A groundbreaking study into football commentary in 2020 found that players with "darker skin tones" are often praised for their athletic abilities, while players with "lighter skin" are regularly and overwhelmingly praised for their hard work and intelligence.[33]

Research show that implicit bias tends to line up with general social hierarchies. The mental shortcuts in your mind are structured by the society you live in, including its inequalities.

RACIAL STEREOTYPES ARE AN EXAMPLE OF IMPLICIT BIAS

A racist stereotype is a fixed, over-generalized belief about a particular racial group. For instance, Mexican people in the USA are stereotyped by some as illegal or uneducated immigrants. This stereotype has travelled worldwide due to Hollywood films repeating this message.

By stereotyping a racial group, you infer that any person belonging to it has a particular range of characteristics and abilities. It prevents you from seeing (and desiring to see) differences between individuals. This serves to perpetuate racism.

Any negative feelings or stereotypes would have been strengthened by a lack of contact with the stereotyped group or any minor negative experience with its members.

WE ARE ALL INDIVIDUALS

By viewing someone as a typical member of a stereotyped group, you are less inclined to put in the effort or time to understand the person as an individual. Even positive stereotypes can be harmful because they rob people of their individuality and put undue pressure on them. Everyone is unique, regardless of their racial group, but lazy stereotypes undermine the important differences and traits between individuals.

Holding racist stereotypes can have ramifications in your actions, without you necessarily realizing it. For instance, if you associate drug dealing with young Black men, then any media representation that affirms this will resonate with you. This belief can make you indifferent if, for instance, you witness a distressed Black schoolboy being searched by police without an adult present.

CULTURAL APPROPRIATION

One practice that can reinforce racial stereotypes is cultural appropriation. This happens when somebody from a dominant culture adopts aspects of another culture that is not their own.

The problem with it stems from the power imbalance: the dominant culture is effectively taking something from an oppressed culture without sufficient respect or appreciation for its value, and a failure to acknowledge its origin. It can suggest a sense of entitlement, as well as a disregard for the needs of the oppressed culture; for instance, wearing a Native American headdress or clothing that depicts the artwork of aboriginal artists.

These actions can reinforce the power imbalance between two cultures, with the appropriator given undue credit for the cultural aspect that they have taken.

EVERYDAY RACISM

Research in Australia shows that the most commonly reported form of racism there is interpersonal racism – that is, interactions between people that maintain and reproduce racial inequality.[34]

One form of this is everyday or "casual" racism, which you might come across on a regular basis. It is usually in the form of "jokes", stereotypes, body language, gestures or expressions. It can be as subtle as restricting eye contact or speaking opportunities to one racial group while excluding another, or it could be as blatant as rudeness, harassment, name-calling or insults. Such displays of racism may occur without any malicious intent and appear harmless. However, the repeated underlying message of inferiority does not go unnoticed by individuals from the targeted racial group.

NATURAL-HAIR DISCRIMINATION

One example of everyday racism is strict policies in schools and workplaces regarding hairstyles. Such policies are usually phrased using terms such as "neat" or "professional" but effectively ban natural Black hair.

In 2020, a survey found that 70 per cent of young Black people in the UK felt pressured to change the natural texture of their hair and the way it grows, in order to be accepted at school or in their jobs.[35]

This discrimination occurs on both sides of the Atlantic. In the USA, there were no laws addressing it until 2019, when the state of California banned discrimination of natural hairstyles (including afros, braids, twists and locks) in the workplace and in schools.

SILENCE

One of the privileges of being white is the option to bypass issues of racism. If racism is discussed, the default response from white people is often (well-intentioned) silence; they simply opt out. Unfortunately, people who are on the receiving end of racism do not have the luxury of that choice.

If you have adopted a strategy of keeping quiet until now, it is time for you to acknowledge that silence reinforces racism. You are not irrelevant to the conversation. While racism can easily be seen as a problem that is too large to overcome, especially by one single person, silence and conformity are what will ensure its continuance. Individual decisions come together to form the collective psyche of society.

TOLERATING RACISM

You may have avoided talking about racism or joining a debate about the issue due to fear of being seen as prejudiced or saying the wrong thing. Social media and "cancel culture" have only served to enhance this fear. The possibility of being misinterpreted, or your words being taken out of context, is an understandable concern. But your silence is not neutral; it has consequences.

Every time you see a small form of racism and decide to stay silent, you bolster your tolerance for racism. From microaggressions and racial slurs, to outright hostility and bias, if these go unchecked, then the capacity for tolerance – yours and other people's – just continues to increase until it eventually leads to devastating events.

UNDERSTANDING WHITE FRAGILITY

White fragility is a term coined to express the common discomfort and clumsiness that white people experience when the issue of racism arises and they are called upon to express their opinions on the matter.

White people are not ordinarily the targets of racism and are therefore sheltered from its direct effects. They have experienced the privileged position of being able to live their life without their race hindering them or being a subject for discussion.

In the USA, surveys show that most young white people value diversity but have only white friends.[36] Consequently, the topic of racism can feel unfamiliar and stressful, leading to denial or defensiveness and continued avoidance of the subject.

"I'M NOT RACIST!"

If you have ever been told that something you said or did was racist and you became defensive, then you need to try to consider why you reacted that way. It is understandable to believe that because your *motives* weren't malicious, then you couldn't have done or said something racist, or harboured prejudices, but this isn't true.

The main reason for taking this defensive attitude is because you have conceptualized racism as extreme and isolated acts of intentional hatred. This narrow definition does not capture the racial inequality that is embedded within society and which has shaped your life – and, inevitably, your biases. Instead of reacting defensively, try to understand and acknowledge the other person's perspective, and consider how you might approach things differently in future.

YOU HAVE THE POWER TO MAKE CHANGE

Racism is an unwanted legacy and, though you didn't create the racial inequalities in society, you do have a role to play in changing them.

If you have adopted the mentality that racism is just too big a problem and there is nothing you can do to change it, then your attitude implies that racism is tolerable and you are powerless. Neither of these statements is true.

Being non-racist is not enough. To dismantle the social structure and systems that support racism, the people *within* the system must take tangible action – and that includes you.

COLOUR-BLIND

Colour blindness is the idea that someone does not "see" colour. They may know this is inaccurate, but they believe it is the correct thing to say. Perhaps you have said or heard the following:

- Discussing race only serves to create or perpetuate racism.
- You do not see colour; you only see the person.
- You do not care if someone is black, brown, white, yellow or purple.

When addressing racism, people often believe that the answer is to treat everyone the same way, regardless of their skin colour, but this is not helpful. It gives the impression that you do not acknowledge or respect the long history of racism, as well as the concerns, problems and traumas that different racial groups experience.

Race categories are not bad in and of themselves. What you need to rally against are the biases and prejudice that come with them.

EXCEPTIONALISM

Like most people, you probably consider yourself a good person.[37] You have never called anyone by a racist slur, and you interact positively with people from a variety of backgrounds. Approaching racism from this perspective is just a form of denial and a way to remove yourself from the conversation.

Acknowledging racism as a problem, and something deserving of your attention, is important. Racism pervades *all* aspects of society. Simply dismissing it as irrelevant to your personal circumstances or your locality, or supposing it only relates to a small minority of racist individuals,[38] ignores the racial inequality within the structures you actively participate in every day.

FIRST STEPS
TO ANTI-RACISM

Being anti-racist means more than just being devoid of racist attitudes and beliefs. To be anti-racist, you are taking responsibility to actively identify, challenge and dismantle the racism you find in your everyday life, including confronting the hard truth of racism within yourself.

This chapter will help you to acknowledge any biases you may hold. This will allow you to start scrutinizing and changing the way you approach both the people who share your racial identity and those who fall into a different category.

The way anti-racism manifests itself will differ from person to person. It depends on who you are, where you live and who you interact with, but the following pages should help you to get started.

WHAT IS ANTI-RACISM?

Anti-racism is an action and a commitment. It is a conscious decision to make frequent, consistent choices every day that promote racial equality, equity and inclusion. Being non-racist is simply an identity, whereas your actions and behaviour are what signal anti-racism.

Though it's important to challenge individual instances of racism, your focus for change should also be on fixing racist policies, customs and procedures. It is looking at where power lies and challenging that.

Before taking such action, you need to make a personal confession. You need to identify any internalized racist ideas and impressions that certain groups are superior to others. You have to become mindful of your own bias and racist stereotypes.

GET MOTIVATED

Anti-racism is a way of life. Like starting any new habit, it requires you to make a conscious decision to pursue it as a regular way of being.

Ask yourself:

- Have you experienced racism or witnessed it? How?
- What is your relationship with people of other races?
- Why does being anti-racist matter to you?
- How will becoming anti-racist change your life?

By being clear about why you want to be anti-racist, you will bring mindful awareness to what you say and do going forward. Setting the intention to have an open mind in order to be anti-racist will inevitably push you beyond your comfort zone and permanently adjust your outlook.

EDUCATE YOURSELF

Education is critical to expanding your awareness of how systemic racism has impacted your life and that of the people around you. By learning about the often unconscious and automatic ways in which racism presents itself, you can start to recognize it and take steps to prevent it.

You should not expect peers or friends from particular racial groups to educate you. There is a plethora of free or easily accessible resources online, as well as books that cost a relatively small price for the astonishing insights that they can provide.

If you find that you have questions that can't seem to be answered, then ask them within relationships that feel safe, and do so respectfully.

ACKNOWLEDGE YOUR BIAS

Work out your beliefs, values and personal biases (see page 46). This includes biases about your own cultural background. One option is taking an Implicit Associations Test (IAT) online. This measures attitudes and beliefs that you may otherwise be unwilling or unable to recognize. Ask yourself: who do you trust in your place of study or work, and why? Do you focus your time or attention toward people who look similar to you? If you were to substitute one acquaintance with another from a different racial group, how would you feel about it?

Once you know and accept that you have bias, you can begin to recognize your own patterns of thinking and start to actively change your thought processes in the future.

REDUCE THE HARM OF YOUR BIAS

If you acknowledge that there is a racial group you automatically avoid or hold less favourably than others, then you can take steps to overcome this. It is not realistic for you to expect to eliminate your bias entirely; the goal is to remove its negative *effects* by revealing and questioning it.

The most powerful way to challenge your bias is to cultivate a fuller and more nuanced perspective of the racial group in question. You can increase your exposure by reading books or watching films by and about people from that group, educating yourself about their culture, and pursuing any opportunities you might have to interact with them.

With awareness and a conscious effort, you can change how you think and challenge the negative or harmful biases you hold.

YOUR FRIEND, MO

Mohamed (and its various spellings) is probably the most common given name in the world. It has appeared in the top 100 boys' names in the UK since 1924. This popularity is, however, not matched with acceptance in Western society.

In a 2017 study by Bristol University, two identical CVs were sent out under the names "Adam" and "Mohamed". Adam was three times more likely to receive a positive response from employers. This is symbolic of a wider issue regarding names: countless famous people, including actors, politicians and TV personalities, have felt compelled to "whiten" their names in order to progress their careers.

Ask yourself: which names do you make assumptions about? Why? Where do your judgments come from?

ACKNOWLEDGE YOUR RACIST STEREOTYPES

Studies show that you can overcome your racial stereotypes, but to do so, you need to first recognize that you have them.

A way to start is by considering the following words and noticing the images that immediately come to mind: cleaner, taxi driver, peaceful protestor, refugee, someone convicted of tax fraud, suicide bomber, someone "looting" a store, religious fundamentalist, drug dealer, violin player, basketball player and pilot. What do you notice about the images you associate with these words?

To be anti-racist, it is critical for you to acknowledge that certain racial groups have been negatively labelled through the media, films, language and the way history has been taught. Trying to suppress or deny the stereotypes in your mind will not work.[39] Instead, consider the possibility that you can observe thoughts without necessarily believing in them.

OVERCOME YOUR STEREOTYPES

There are a number of ways you can help yourself to move beyond racial stereotypes and the resulting racial inequality you have in your mind.

One technique is to actively try to replace your stereotypes with an unbiased response. When you notice yourself reacting in a particular way or making impulsive judgments based on someone's race, label that response as stereotyping. You could start by trying this for one week and maybe even keeping a journal so that you can spot any patterns in your thinking.

This will allow you to question why you respond in this way and will start a mental process of dismantling your racial assumptions. With consistent reflection like this, you can begin to notice a change in your reactions, where you merely *observe* your stereotypes rather than acting on them.

You can also start counteracting your stereotypes with alternative images. For instance, if you notice a tendency to associate Black men with criminality or being absent father figures then look for different examples. Use social media to follow people that offset the typical images you see, such as Black classical musicians, artists, scientists or brilliant fathers. This might start to rewire your automatic associations.

You could expand your social and professional circles to people of other racial and cultural backgrounds, or deepen the relationships you already have. Perhaps you will need to be bold and start conversations. The important thing is to search for commonalities rather than differences.

If you find yourself continuing to have judgements or pre-conceived ideas about people from certain racial groups, then consciously think of evidence that disproves your stereotypes.

IT'S OKAY TO MAKE MISTAKES

It is an understandable fear that you might say the wrong thing or unintentionally offend someone in your anti-racism efforts. However, by focusing on your own intent and feelings, or your own image, you are inadvertently practising the belief that your potential discomfort matters more than the very real pain that racism inflicts on others.

Don't let the fear of making mistakes be a deterrent to taking action, otherwise your anti-racism efforts will become stalled by perfectionism. You need to accept that mistakes are likely and are in fact something to be welcomed; they signal an opportunity for education and growth.

WORKING ON EMPATHY

Empathy is the ability to understand and share the feelings of another person. Studies show that it is key to creating connection and breaking down any notions of "us versus them". Part of the reason why racism has persisted for so long is because society's value system has not prioritized empathy.

The global "Black Lives Matter" protests of 2020 demonstrated the power of empathy. Thousands of people around the world, from different racial groups, marched alongside Black people because they were able to understand and rationalize the impact of racism toward Black people in particular, especially in the context of police brutality. They shared their sense of grief, anger and injustice.

Cultivating empathy, and having the courage to *show* your empathy, is key to rehumanizing the dehumanized and achieving racial equality.

AN ALTERNATIVE PERSPECTIVE

Studies suggest that putting yourself in another person's shoes can significantly reduce your unconscious bias, and consequently improve your real-world interactions with people of different races.[40]

Reading literature by writers from diverse backgrounds can help with this. You could challenge yourself to read a certain number of books or articles in a year by authors from a different racial background.

An Australian smartphone app, named Everyday Racism, challenges players to spend a week receiving texts, tweets, images and videos that will give them an insight into what life is like as an Aboriginal man, a Muslim woman or an Indian student. It provides an immersive experience that will challenge your assumptions and help to increase your empathy for those targeted by racism.

If you prefer pen and paper, there are websites that can help you to find an international pen pal, such as www.interpals.net.

TIME TO HEAL

Racial Healing Circles are short group meetings with 8–12 participants, aiming to raise each other's awareness, consciousness and empathy regarding racism. The confidential and sympathetic setting allows participants to be frank about their personal experiences and biases.

Consider joining or setting up one of these circles in your area. It might assist your process of self-reflection, and provide a non-threatening environment to acknowledge and start dismantling any racist ideas or bias you discover in yourself.

While these circles are not specifically about anti-racism, talking openly and listening to the stories of others might help to open yourself up to people from different backgrounds and develop greater empathy.

"WHERE ARE YOU FROM?"

It's common knowledge that you should avoid discussing politics, religion or money when you first meet someone, but you should also be wary of asking about a person's race, origin or ethnicity.

While it may seem innocuous, the question "Where are you from?" is likely to have been heard by the recipient on hundreds of occasions. Repeated time and again, it makes the person you're talking to feel that they are outside the norm and that they will forever be considered a "foreigner".

If the question crosses your mind, don't enquire in what appears to be a casual manner. They may choose to offer up that information, but if they don't, don't ask. Though curiosity is a virtue, insensitivity is not.

EMBRACE YOUR DISCOMFORT

Facing facts about white privilege, your bias and racial stereotypes is a challenge. You have to be honest, vulnerable and willing to see your weaknesses. Being aware that systemic racism may have benefited you at the expense of other people, even if you were oblivious to it, may bring uncomfortable feelings of guilt, shame or anger.

This discomfort should be welcomed, as it is a sign of insight and inherent change. Without this internal shift, you cannot make any external change. Growth begins where comfort ends.

To be anti-racist, you have to prioritize courage, compassion and vulnerability over your own comfort or ease. By choosing to acknowledge your weaknesses and be courageous, you can begin to inspire collective action and change.

TRAIN YOUR BRAIN

You might be wondering whether you can overcome the racial bias that your mind has accumulated throughout your life, particularly if society keeps repeating those messages back to you.

Fortunately, studies confirm that you can reconfigure your unconscious judgments. You have the benefit of "neuroplasticity": a malleable brain that can structurally and functionally change through new experiences. By actively exposing yourself to new stimuli and alternative associations (see page 72), you can create neural pathways that will restructure any old and rigid belief systems.[41]

You can also control your impulsive reactions through cognitive exercises, like focused breathing and meditation. When you're overwhelmed, you are more likely to make snap judgments; by reducing your stress and cognitive load, your brain is less likely to rely on its biases. A 2016 study found that brief meditation practices reduced the participants' unconscious bias against Black people.[42]

YOUR VALUES

As you embark on your anti-racism work, it is worth taking the time to reconsider your core values, bearing in mind the following:

- Self-compassion – you cannot grow if you get stuck in guilt or shame for any privilege you have benefited from, or any racist ideas you have unwittingly absorbed.

- Sympathy – for your peers who might also harbour unconscious biases and unwittingly express these in their actions.

- Compassion – for people on the receiving end of racism. You are not their "saviour"; you need to listen and stand in kinship with them, so that you can cooperate in creating a future without racism.

- Courage – be bold and brave in tackling racism. Be clear in your mind that change *is* necessary, the elimination of racism *is* possible and your actions (not your inactions) *will* make a difference.

- Consciousness – be mindful of what you say and do.

- Commitment – anti-racism is a lifetime of action. You will need to persevere even when faced with (inevitable) challenges.

HOW TO BE
AN ALLY

It is likely that you saw, or even posted, black squares on your social media accounts during the "Black Lives Matter" protests in 2020. You may have read articles about racism and attended "diversity and inclusion" training. As important as these actions have been, they are not enough to dismantle racism.

If you are fortunate enough to have never experienced racism, or your circumstances now shield you from it, then you effectively hold a powerful position within the social structure, which can be utilized to further racial equality, equity and inclusion.

This chapter contains tips that will help you to be a lifelong ally to people who experience racism, and to take on their struggle as your own. It is not a comprehensive list but rather a useful steer to direct your personal path to effective allyship.

WHAT IS AN ALLY?

An ally is someone who is involved in an ongoing process of supporting a group they are not a member of. In the context of racism, an ally is anyone who actively works to create and promote racial equality. To be an ally, you have to make a concerted effort to improve your understanding of the various forms of racism and consequent obstacles that people face.

Anyone has the potential to be an ally; being a member of a racial group that isn't marginalized does not prevent you from being an ally and it certainly does not limit the potential impact of your work. On the contrary, the greater privilege you have in society, the more powerful your voice will be in standing alongside marginalized ones.

OPTICAL AND NON-OPTICAL ALLYSHIP

Optical allyship (sometimes called performative allyship) is action or behaviour that only serves to benefit your self-image. Instead, we need to strive for non-optical allyship.

You should not expect to be acknowledged, complimented or rewarded for taking action against racism. It is important to remember that your goal is not to feel good about yourself or to simply copy trends on social media. Your goal is to educate yourself and the people around you to effect change.

Allyship is an opportunity to learn, show courage and reach out to those who would benefit from your help in challenging injustice and racial inequality. It is not tokenism or momentary allegiance; it is a continual commitment to learn, reflect and grow.

LISTEN MORE, TALK LESS

The term "whitesplaining" refers to conversations between a white person and a non-white person, where the latter is talking about racism. Whitesplaining is when the white person explains something despite having no experience about the matter being discussed, causing the non-white person to feel ignored and silenced. An example might be an Indian man retelling an experience of racism and a white man interrupting by mentioning a book he has read by an Indian author and what he learned about racism.

We need to avoid this kind of response-driven interaction and instead learn to be active listeners. Show your openness to learning by listening with the specific intention to connect and understand. Do not try to disprove or find holes in people's stories; acknowledge that you do not have all the answers. Exercise humility, and recognize that living with racism and observing racism are two very different things.

EXERCISE SELF-AWARENESS

It can be easy to go through life disregarding otherwise questionable situations, such as a lack of diversity in your friendship circle or your workplace, or even racism within your own family. One way to avoid this complacency is to practise self-awareness and systemic awareness.

Consider the following:

- Where do you buy your groceries and clothing? Who cuts your hair?
- Your favourite musicians, authors, artists, directors, actors – are they largely (or solely) from one racial group?
- Do you know a family member or friend who makes racist comments?
- How diverse is your neighbourhood, friendship circle, workplace?

By becoming aware of yourself in a way that challenges what you have always assumed to be true or acceptable, you can recognize your privileges and potential contribution as an ally.

ADOPT A "GROWTH MINDSET"

There is a theory in psychology that we have either a "fixed mindset" or a "growth mindset". The former assumes that our character and ability are basically determined at birth, while a "growth mindset" believes that a person's potential is unknown, and we can grow and change through our efforts and challenges.

To be an effective ally, you need to adopt a "growth mindset", and admit that you have a lot to learn and unlearn. Instead of seeking the approval of others, show that you are aware of your unconscious biases and that you are actively re-educating yourself (for example, create opportunities for discussion and recommend the relevant books you are reading). This can build trust with people that you hope to assist.

By adopting a "growth mindset", you will also be better equipped to recover from any mistakes you make and to take responsibility.

RECOGNIZE DIVERSITY

It's essential that we all understand that there are variations between different racial groups (as well as within each one), rather than grouping them all together. For instance, a Pakistani woman, a Mexican man and a Black woman would face different types of discrimination and stereotyping, and people who share the same racial group will also have different individual life experiences. This highlights the importance again of listening with an open mind to each person's story.

To be an effective ally, you need to appreciate the diversity of racist experiences across and within racial groups. Show that you acknowledge this variety by listening carefully and asking questions that relate to individual circumstances.

GET COMFORTABLE

You need to get comfortable talking about race and racism. Hiding behind words such as "diversity" or "inclusion" will limit the reach of any conversation.

Whenever you're in a position to have an open and frank discussion about racism, try something like: "Race is challenging to talk about, but I will try my best. Tell me if something I say comes across as insensitive or offensive, as that is not my intention."

Educate yourself as to what terminology is appropriate at any given time or place. For instance, in 2020 the most common acronyms for non-white racial groups were BIPOC (Black, Indigenous, People of Color) in North America and BAME (Black, Asian, Minority Ethnic) in the UK, but these terms are not perfect and many people find them problematic. The language around race and racism is ever-evolving, so it is important to acknowledge any controversies surrounding terms and to stay informed.

YOU WILL BE WRONG

You may be unwilling or nervous about being a visible ally, in case you say something wrong. Unfortunately, there is no guarantee against this, as your words and actions are inherently shaped and influenced by systemic racism. This means that there is much to unlearn and learn, and mistakes are expected.

As an ally, you need to acknowledge any errors you make, take responsibility and be proactive in your education. As long as you're learning from your mistakes, you're on the right path.

CHALLENGE BIAS

As you become more alert to racism in your daily life and interactions, you will inevitably come across other people's unconscious biases, as well as possible explicit forms of racism. It can be particularly challenging to confront racist jokes or bias among family or friends. You can try letting people know that you feel uncomfortable and you'd rather they didn't make comments like that around you. Some things you can say:

- "I've heard/experienced something different."
- "Do you think there are other opinions?"
- "Where did you hear that?"
- "That's not right."
- Explain (calmly) why you disagree.

You cannot overcome people's biases in just one conversation, but at least you can establish your boundaries around certain topics and potentially inspire a process of reflection for others.

WHAT TO DO WHEN YOU WITNESS RACISM

If you encounter someone being racist, have the courage to constructively challenge the person or prevent the situation from escalating.

The priority is that you remain calm. Rather than becoming angry, try to approach the person who is being racist with a composed demeanour. This will be much more productive and prevent the individual from reacting defensively.

Ask the person why they have that particular point of view and offer an alternative perspective. If the target of the racism is present, check that they are safe and unharmed, show your empathy, and ask them if they would like any help.

If necessary, take notes or record the incident and report it to the police.

HOW TO SUPPORT PEOPLE EXPERIENCING RACISM

As well as the physical harm and devastation that violent racism can inflict, verbal and systemic forms of racism also have real, traumatic consequences – not least making the target feel humiliated, threatened and alone.

If you have a friend or peer who experiences racism in any form, show that you support them and that you are on their side. Make the effort to have a one-on-one conversation if you've witnessed a person being targeted or you know they have been targeted in the past. Show them that you are available to listen if they want to talk about it. Make it clear that you stand with them and not the oppressor.

BEWARE WHAT YOU SHARE

Be mindful of sharing traumatic news stories, videos and images of racism (particularly without a trigger warning). These often serve to further dehumanize and upset members of the same racial group and others who experience racism. There are many other ways to bring awareness and to make a point without repeating the "victim" narrative over and over again.

If you get into a discussion about racism, perhaps with your friends or online, showcase the opinions of those who are experiencing it rather than your own thoughts, using your platform to amplify the voices of non-white people. Share an article, post or video by someone of that race, rather than your own, so that their views can be heard by a wider audience.

ADVOCATE FOR CHANGE

In order to be an effective ally and elicit change, you need to be a visible advocate for racial equality.

As an individual, talk openly about anti-racism with your friends and encourage them to do the same. Share informative and educational articles on social media or create your own posts on the topic, perhaps about the practical steps you are taking to bring about racial equality within your daily life.

You can also advocate as part of a collective; for example, you could join diversity and inclusion groups or volunteer for organizations that have anti-racism objectives. Look for local initiatives or events that you can get involved in.

THE CHILDREN ARE OUR FUTURE

Talking to young children about race can reduce the chances of them becoming racially biased in later life. If the topic of race comes up, keep the conversation as simple as possible and try the following:

- Don't be afraid to acknowledge and celebrate physical differences, such as skin tone and hair types, but make sure you balance it by talking about the characteristics we all share, too.
- Compare the child's skin tone with yours and point out unique traits, such as birthmarks.
- Explain that touching someone's clothing or body is not polite, unless you know them well enough to ask their permission.
- If appropriate, talk about the child's family history and where their ancestors come from.
- Ask them about their friends who may be from different races, ethnicities and cultures.
- If appropriate, let them know what is and is not acceptable behaviour, and explain why racism is wrong.
- Respond positively to questions.

AN ALLY IN THE WORKPLACE

Diversity and inclusion efforts are visible in all sorts of workplaces, but it is questionable whether they are making a tangible difference. Employers and managers may have the best of intentions, but no concept of how to encourage racial equality within their specific environment.

Regardless of your job or position in the hierarchy of an organization, you can work to encourage positive change. Anti-racism needs to be an ethos championed by both management and the entire workplace, so that its importance is clear. You can find tips on how to do this in the next few pages.

Bear in mind that you should speak on behalf of the values and strategy of the workplace, not on behalf of a racial group.

TIPS FOR EMPLOYERS

To overcome widespread racial differences in hiring, performance ratings, promotions and retention, employers and those in management positions can try the following:

- Think more creatively about how and where you recruit from. Open up new avenues for people from marginalized backgrounds to find and apply for jobs.
- Ensure that the accomplishments of non-white employees are recognized and that they are put forward for promotions.
- Conduct (mandatory) anti-bias and cultural competence training.
- Encourage open discussions about race specifically (led by people that are suitably trained), and amplify the voices of non-white employees to ensure everyone feels heard and supported.
- Support mentorship initiatives.
- Measure diversity and inclusion efforts in performance evaluations, link them to salary increases or bonuses, and praise employees who demonstrate inclusive values.
- Emphasize the value of a workplace that embraces all styles and behaviours.

TIPS FOR EMPLOYEES

As an employee, speak up immediately if you witness racist behaviour in your workplace. Staying silent will condone it and allow it to continue.

Hold your employer and managers accountable for progress toward your organization's diversity and inclusion goals.

Look at your workplace policies and culture, and interrogate seemingly mundane practices, such as whether there is space (or time permitted) for religious worship, the dress and hair policy, attitudes to different cultural or religious holidays, and so on.

If your workplace has a diversity or inclusion network, ask if they have articles or materials that are relevant to your industry and that can help you learn more about being an effective ally.

AMPLIFY MARGINALIZED VOICES

Representation is a key step toward racial equality. We know that the language used by the media and biased reporters can skew all of our perspectives and biases (see pages 36 and 48). Non-white people need to have the platform to tell their stories in their own words.

Some possible ways to encourage this are as follows:

- If you're asked to speak or contribute to an event that doesn't include any (or not enough) non-white speakers, you could respond to the organizers to say you'd prefer for your seat to go to a non-white person.
- If you're given or have created a platform, invite non-white colleagues/friends/contacts to use it to promote their own work.

By taking steps like this, you can use any privileged position you have to boost the voices of non-white people that might otherwise be marginalized.

SELF-CARE

Being an ally will bring up difficulties. Observing and directly confronting racism, hearing stories of racist incidents, and actively discussing the topic may be stressful and overwhelming at times.

In order to contribute to anti-racism efforts and be an effective ally, you must also look after your own needs, particularly your mental health and resilience. Take time to rest, meditate or relax in the ways that work for you, so that you can give the work of allyship the attention and care it needs. If you need to, discuss any problems you're encountering with other allies who can relate to what you are going through.

ALLY DOs

- Do read widely and educate yourself.
- Do confront your implicit biases.
- Do exercise self-awareness and self-compassion to acknowledge your role within the social structure of racism.
- Do recognize inequality and the various ways it's shown, such as microaggressions.
- Do exercise humility, accept criticism and admit your mistakes, regardless of any discomfort you might have.
- Do reflect on how to change the social systems that sustain inequality.
- Do be open to active listening.
- Do believe and appreciate the experience of others.
- Do use any privilege you have to amplify marginalized voices.
- Do commit yourself to be a better ally every day.

ALLY DON'Ts

- Do not feel insignificant; social change starts with the individual.
- Do not expect to be educated by your peers.
- Do not expect to be praised.
- Do not act only if there is a particular audience.
- Do not make comparisons with struggles in your own life; racism is a distinct experience.
- Do not use your voice or power at the expense of others, or assume that you know best.
- Do not thoughtlessly share images or videos of racist violence on social media.
- Do not talk about recipients of racism as "victims".
- Do not assume that all racial groups experience the same forms of racism.
- Do not neglect your well-being and mental health needs.[43]

SUPPORTING
AN ANTI-RACIST
SOCIETY

Albert Einstein said, "We cannot solve our problems
with the same thinking we used when we created
them." The fact that the initial problem of racism
was, of course, not created by you or anyone
living today allows for innovative solutions
and sweeping social reform – if we want it.

This chapter sets out a vision for some of
the ideas and actions you can champion
as part of the anti-racism movement.

You do not need to be an extrovert or to have
a public profile. If you are a quieter person,
you can still use the tools at your disposal to
inspire change. Your support is not measured
by your volume or your popularity; it is in
your personal and everyday choices.

THINK OF FUTURE GENERATIONS

We all need to disregard the idea that racism is a problem too big to overcome. Every little action taken to counteract racism can inspire more people to do the same and will move us all forward in the right direction. While full racial equality may not be achieved in our lifetime, progress toward that end certainly can.

Consider the people living in the early twentieth century who had the audacity to believe that one day women would be equal to men in their education, suffrage, career options, inheritance rights, and so on. Yes, full gender equality is not here yet, but there is no denying the progress that continues to be made. And it started with the belief that it was possible.

PEOPLE ARE THE SOLUTION

When trying to enact change in your workplace or in an organization, don't dwell on the size and power of the institution. This will only intimidate you and make you feel insignificant in comparison. Remember: a system is not amorphous; it is made up of people.

Search for the individuals within an institution or system that are responsible for policy creation or compliance and try to send an email or address a letter to their office. Explain your concerns about their policies or cultures that perpetuate racism. Ask them how a racist practice can be justified in light of diversity and inclusion goals, an institution's values and racial equality in general. This should not be phrased as a personal attack but as a policy observation. To inspire change, avoid a defensive reaction by instigating a productive conversation.

ENACTING CHANGE IN EDUCATION

There are countless ways in which educational establishments can reinforce or diminish racial inequality. The content of what is being taught is a key issue, with calls to "decolonize the curriculum" having been made by students from various universities since 2015. There are diverse views about what this would mean in practice, with the debate also raising questions about representation in the teaching profession, and the way subjects are taught and assessed.

If you or someone you know attend a school, college or university, think critically about whether its current policies support anti-racism. Consider: the curriculum, staff diversity, grading systems, textbooks and literature (authors and content), standardized tests, scholarships/grants, guidance or careers counsellors, mentorship, and how to bridge any opportunity gaps for non-white students. Discuss your thoughts with other students and present them to the institution's leaders.

CHILDREN'S SETTINGS

If children do not grow up observing examples of racial equality and actively being taught how to be anti-racist, then they will absorb the same biases and racial stereotypes that dominate society. In any relationship you have with a child, consider how the issue of race is being presented to them.

At home, nursery, children's libraries, play centres and school, visual images should be devoid of stereotypes and balanced in their racial representation. Children need racial "mirrors and windows":[44] reflections of themselves to feel seen, validated and inspired, and windows to the wider world to understand diversity, increase empathy and enhance creativity.

Toys and books that celebrate diversity, as well as songs, dances or cuisine from different cultures, are gentle ways to introduce the topic (see "Further resources", pages 124–5).

VOTE!

Use your right to vote, in every form of election available to you, to support individuals that champion anti-racist policies.

Identify candidates' stances with regard to education, healthcare, housing, policing and any other areas you are passionate about in the specific context of racial equality. Support candidates who tackle inequality and aim to dismantle or transform existing racist policies, and engage others in conversation about them. You could even volunteer by flyering or making sure people are registered to vote.

Consider the candidates themselves. Are they all from one racial group and if so, why? Is it because no one else is qualified or willing to stand, or is there a policy causing this?

Share what you discover with your social and professional circles so that others can take anti-racism into account when they vote.

THE POWER OF PROTESTS

In May 2020, the death of an unarmed Black man, George Floyd, by a police officer kneeling on his neck caused over seven million people to protest in the USA. The outcry spread to Australia, Canada and European states, despite the Covid-19 pandemic raging at the time.

Protests can catalyze self-reflection, public debate and systemic change. As well as the removal of racist statues, these mass demonstrations immediately led to a civil rights and police reform bill being drafted in the US Congress, and to wider discussions about defunding the police in the USA.

Participating in protests, marches, rallies and boycotts is an important way to show your support for anti-racism. This kind of action can drive media coverage, as well as shifting attitudes and public opinion in favour of anti-racism, and thereby forcing necessary local and national policy changes.

HOLD PUBLIC OFFICIALS ACCOUNTABLE

Public officials who use excessive force or who racially profile people need to be made accountable for their actions. This applies to police officers, as well as airport security, border agency staff, security guards, and so on.

Look for and disseminate ways to increase their accountability. One example is Legal Lifelines, a free app that allows anyone stopped and searched by police to film incidents to ensure that they have an "independent witness". Footage is uploaded in real time to the cloud, using military-grade encryption, thus preserving it even if the phone is damaged or confiscated. By raising awareness about initiatives like this, you can help to increase accountability, and thereby decrease the incidence of excessive force and police brutality.

You could also research the rights that people have when questioned by police and other officials in your country, and raise awareness by sharing the information you find on social media or through community organizations.

YOUR COMMUNITY

Make a commitment to your local community to enhance racial equality.

Perhaps you can get involved in local government or forums and community groups, so you'll be better placed to raise issues or opportunities for greater racial diversity and inclusion when they arise. Consider things such as festivals, advertisements, celebrations and new projects from an anti-racist perspective. You can then raise any issues you may come across for debate at local meetings or contact your local representatives and make them accountable for their decisions, if applicable. A number of anti-racism organizations provide template letters or emails for you to use.

It is possible that racial bias has simply been overlooked. Raising awareness will be helpful to the representatives, as well as the residents, in your area.

MONEY TALKS

To support a diverse society, buy more services and products from non-white-owned businesses. This will help to create opportunities and mitigate the systemic racism of banks (that are less likely to give loans or credit cards to Black-owned businesses).

As a consumer, you have power in choosing where and how you spend your money. In support of anti-racism, you can make a tangible difference by shopping mindfully and searching for independent businesses that are owned by people from marginalized racial groups. Make an effort to avoid businesses whose practices do not align with anti-racist values.

Sources to help you discover and support businesses include: Beyond Buckskin, "Black Pound Day" (in the UK), Blaqbase app, Supply Nation, Wakuda app, Shoppe Black and Amnesty International shop.

INCLUSIVE ECONOMY

Part of creating an anti-racist society is shifting the flow of money to corporations with diverse leadership, and which incorporate diversity goals and anti-racism measures in their policies and practices.

Think about what you own and where you bank from an anti-racism perspective. Choose an establishment that grants loans to non-white entrepreneurs or that works to enhance financial literacy among disadvantaged youths. Your deposits and retirement funds are being loaned out by the bank for other purposes – make sure that those loans align with your values.

If you own shares, look at the leadership in those companies to ensure diversity and check whether they have measurable anti-racism policies. If not, communicate your concerns or invest elsewhere. Prioritize justice and ethical values over profit.

CULTURE SHIFT

Studies show that white people are more likely to view a film with a non-white cast if it is recommended to them by another white person,[45] and both Black and white audiences in the USA are averse to watching foreign films with subtitles.[46]

To combat this, when selecting a movie, book, TV show, documentary, exhibition or any other form of entertainment, choose something that is not predominantly made by or starring people who share your racial group. Put aside any perception that you are not the target audience and instead try a new experience with an open mind.

Make it a habit to always recommend your discoveries to friends and family, especially those who are reluctant to try something different.

SWITCH OFF RACISM

If you find yourself watching a film or TV show that is reinforcing racial stereotypes, switch it off. Better still, tell all your friends and followers why they should not watch it either. The same principle applies to racially biased newspapers, magazines and product advertisements.

The media has played an instrumental role in forming society's collective racial bias and stereotypes. One powerful way to stop the same ideas circulating, and repeating, for future generations is to withdraw your attention and money.

If audience figures, readership and profits go down, those in charge will be obligated to reflect on their racial bias and permanently change their approach.

DONATE

Charitable organizations led by non-white people receive less money than those led by white people. In the USA, when looking at organizations that support Black boys to improve their prospects, those that are led by Black leaders receive 45 per cent less revenue than their counterparts with white leaders.[47] This means that charitable giving can inadvertently reinforce racial inequality.

A simple way to support anti-racism is to donate money to racial justice organizations. Examples include: The Movement for Black Lives, NAACP, Black Youth Project (USA), All Together Now, Centre for Multicultural Youth (Australia), Circles for Reconciliation, Across Boundaries (Canada), Show Racism the Red Card and Blueprint for All (UK). Directing your charitable giving in this way can make a tangible difference, particularly if you form a regular habit.

DEDICATE TIME

Aside from donations, there are many ways you can support the work of anti-racist organizations.

You could become a member of a charity or group and volunteer your time on a regular basis to help their fundraising efforts. Use any privilege and networks you have to raise awareness of their work and campaigns.

You could coordinate mandatory anti-racism training in your place of study or work, and identify suitable diversity and inclusion consultants to conduct it. External consultants can help to start uncomfortable conversations, create a common baseline understanding and help in formulating new inclusive strategies.

You could sign petitions regarding anti-racism policies. Petitions can relate to demanding the arrest of officers involved in police brutality, mandating anti-racism education, removing monuments, etc. Whatever you do, by donating your time you will be helping to create positive change.

TACKLING TECHNO-RACISM

Since 2019, there has been a growing "tech justice" movement that is seeking to incorporate anti-racism in the way technology is created and implemented.[48] Diversity and progressive thinking within technology companies is not enough to overcome the effects of unconscious racial biases and oversight, such as facial analysis algorithms misclassifying Black women at far greater rates than white men.[49]

If you discover racial bias in the *design* or *outcomes* of the technology you use, you can report it to the technology company directly or open-source tools such as AI Fairness 360. For instance, perhaps a dating app only matches you with people that share your racial identity, or a camera does not capture darker skin tones as well as lighter skin tones.

If you come across a website that is racist, or supports violence, then contact the hosting company, as it is likely that this breaches its policies. Alternatively, you can report it through organizations like the Online Hate Prevention Institute.

SHUTTING DOWN RACISM ON SOCIAL MEDIA

If someone you follow on social media posts something that seems racially biased, consider talking to them privately to understand the wider context and tailor your response.

If you want to comment publicly in response to a sweeping generalization or stereotype that has been stated, consider providing a contradictory fact to challenge the person's assumptions. Try to stay calm and measured in your response, as arguing won't help anyone.

If necessary, report it – just look for the "Contact us" page or "Report this" button. Reporting helps platforms to recognize racist expressions that moderators might not understand or that algorithms fail to identify. Do not spread hate or give greater attention to extremist content; focus on stopping it.

If you come across illegal hate content that originates in your country, you can also report it to the police.

BE YOUR OWN GATEKEEPER

You, as a social media consumer, need to be aware that algorithms cause your biases to be reflected and repeated back to you. To avoid an echo chamber effect (where you only see your own beliefs and values repeated and reinforced by people from similar backgrounds), you need to take as much control as you can and ignore (or at least take with a pinch of salt) the friend recommendations, advertisements and news stories that appear on your social media feeds.

Instead of being an apathetic user, actively work to diversify your social media feeds. Search for and follow people from different racial groups, as well as anti-racism advocates. You could start by following well-known actors, artists, sports people, writers or organizations that advocate racial equality and anti-racism. Make an effort to overcome any biases you hold and follow accounts that contradict them.

LEAD BY EXAMPLE

The flip side of your work to suppress racism in society is to *elevate* the voices of anti-racists and those subjected to racism.

Share what you learn about ways or reasons to promote racial inclusion in society. Recommend books, films or documentaries that are insightful or that show life from a different racial perspective.

Actively and consistently raise the visibility of individuals from diverse backgrounds. Make this a habit whenever you come across someone from an under-represented racial group who inspires you, or whose work and life run contrary to the common stereotypes of their racial group.

If you are the first to do this among your friends, you will open doors for others to follow.

CONCLUSION

The house that racism built is the house we all grew up in. From your education, the TV you watch and the adverts you see, to the news you read, society has taught us to group people into categories and associate those groups with stereotypes.

You stand at a precipice in history, when swathes of people across the world are rejecting this social framework and demanding a future that is built on historical awareness, reflection and compassion.

A fundamentally different kind of world can be envisaged because the tools to achieve it are now commonly available. Through platforms that unite ideas across borders and knowledge that can transfer without institutional barriers, people are realizing why we should say no to racism and how we can evolve beyond it.

By adding your voice to this collective effort, the vast construction of racism can be one knock closer to finally toppling.

FURTHER RESOURCES

BOOKS TO READ:

- Akala, *Natives: Race and Class in the Ruins of Empire* (2019)
- Angela Saini, *Superior: The Return of Race Science* (2019)
- David Olusoga, *Black and British: A Forgotten History* (2016)
- Ibram X. Kendi, *How to Be an Antiracist* (2019)
- Ijeoma Oluo, *So You Want to Talk About Race* (2018)
- Jennifer Eberhardt, *Biased: Uncovering the Hidden Prejudices That Shape Our Lives* (2020)
- Nikesh Shukla, *The Good Immigrant* (2017)
- Pragya Agarwal, *Sway: Unravelling Unconscious Bias* (2020)
- Priya Satia, *Time's Monster: History, Conscience and Britain's Empire* (2020)
- Reni Eddo-Lodge, *Why I'm No Longer Talking to White People About Race* (2017)
- Sathnam Sanghera, *Empireland: How Imperialism Has Shaped Modern Britain* (2021)
- Toni Morrison, *The Origin of Others* (2017)

WHAT TO WATCH:

- *12 Years A Slave* (2013, Steve McQueen)
- *American History X* (1998, Tony Kaye)
- *BlacKkKlansman* (2018, Spike Lee)
- *East Is East* (1999, Damien O'Donnell)
- *Gran Torino* (2008, Clint Eastwood)
- *I Am Not Your Negro* (2016, Raoul Peck)
- *Little Fires Everywhere* (2020, Lynn Shelton)
- *The Post-Racist Planet* (2020, VPRO documentary)
- *The Problem with Apu* (2017, Michael Melamedoff)
- *When They See Us* (2019, Ava DuVernay)

BOOKS FOR KIDS:

- Alexandra Penfold, *All Are Welcome* (2018)
- Anna Forgerson Hindley, *A is for All the Things You Are: A Joyful ABC Book* (2019)
- Jasmine Warga, *Other Words for Home* (2019)
- Sharee Miller, *Don't Touch My Hair!* (2018)
- Tiffany Jewell, *This Book Is Anti-Racist: 20 Lessons on how to Wake Up, Take Action, and Do the Work* (2020)
- Trevor Noah, *Born a Crime: Stories from a South African Childhood (Adapted for Young Readers)* (2019)
- Yamile Saied Méndez, *Where Are You From?* (2019)

FOOTNOTES

1 www.britannica.com/topic/race-human/The-history-of-the-idea-of-race

2 www.history.com/news/the-grisly-story-of-americas-largest-lynching

3 andrewleigh.org//pdf/AuditDiscrimination.pdf

4 www.imf.org/external/pubs/ft/fandd/2020/09/the-economic-cost-of-racism-losavio.htm

5 www.huffingtonpost.co.uk/entry/racial-disparities-criminal-justice_n_4045144

6 www.sentencingproject.org/publications/locked-out-2020-estimates-of-people-denied-voting-rights-due-to-a-felony-conviction/

7 www.theguardian.com/law/2019/may/04/stop-and-search-new-row-racial-bias

8 www.theguardian.com/australia-news/2020/jun/16/nsw-police-disproportionately-target-indigenous-people-in-strip-searches

9 www.imf.org/external/pubs/ft/fandd/2020/09/the-economic-cost-of-racism-losavio.htm

10 www.healthline.com/health/this-is-what-its-like-to-navigate-healthcare-while-black#My-[white]-friends-got-the-mono-test-right-away

11 www.statnews.com/2020/06/09/systemic-racism-black-health-disparities/

12 www.theguardian.com/world/2020/may/07/black-people-four-times-more-likely-to-die-from-covid-19-ons-finds

13 www.livescience.com/difference-between-race-ethnicity.html

14 www.theguardian.com/media/2020/jan/26/migrants-are-off-the-agenda-for-the-uk-press-but-the-damage-is-done

15 www.aljazeera.com/news/2020/11/16/hate-crimes-rise-to-10-year-high-killings-highest-ever-fbi

16 www.naacp.org/criminal-justice-fact-sheet/

17 www.naacp.org/criminal-justice-fact-sheet/

18 eu.usatoday.com/story/news/nation/2021/01/06/us-capitol-attack-compared-response-black-lives-matter-protests/6570528002/

19 www.nytimes.com/2021/01/07/us/capitol-trump-mob-black-lives-matter.html

20 digitalcommons.mainelaw.maine.edu/cgi/viewcontent.cgi?article=1007&context=faculty-publications

21 www.washingtonpost.com/education/2019/08/28/teaching-slavery-schools/?arc404=true

22 www.cbc.ca/news/indigenous/indigenous-content-school-curriculums-trc-1.5300580

23 www.theguardian.com/books/2019/apr/15/fewer-than-2-of-british-childrens-authors-are-people-of-colour

24 www.opportunityagenda.org/explore/resources-publications/media-representations-impact-black-men/media-portrayals

25 www.equity.org.uk/media/4062/equity_diversity_guide_2020-v3-sp.pdf

26 See footnote 24

27 theconversation.com/the-hypocritical-media-coverage-of-the-new-zealand-terror-attacks-113713

28 criticalmediaproject.org/bias-in-mainstream-news/

29 www.theguardian.com/us-news/2018/jul/20/muslim-terror-attacks-press-coverage-study

30 www.computerweekly.com/news/252489419/Twitter-investigates-image-cropping-algorithm-for-racial-bias

31 ucc.nd.edu/self-help/multicultural-awareness/overcoming-stereotypes/

32 www.simplypsychology.org/implicit-bias.html

33 runrepeat.com/racial-bias-study-soccer

34 theconversation.com/explainer-what-is-casual-racism-30464

35 www.theguardian.com/world/2020/oct/29/most-black-british-children-report-experiencing-racism-at-school

36 www.bbc.co.uk/news/world-us-canada-30214825

37 www.independent.co.uk/life-style/people-think-nicer-reality-self-image-see-yourself-goldsmiths-university-monarch-a7627161.html

38 www.academia.edu/3526619/Denial_of_racism_and_its_implications_for_local_action_draft_only_

39 www.psychologytoday.com/gb/blog/culturally-speaking/201608/exploring-our-own-stereotypes-and-biases

40 greatergood.berkeley.edu/article/item/empathy_reduces_racism

41 www.psychologytoday.com/gb/blog/mind-in-the-machine/201809/understanding-the-racist-brain

42 www.researchgate.net/publication/294276984_Brief_Mindfulness_Meditation_Reduces_Discrimination

43 Ally lists inspired by https://guidetoallyship.com by Amélie Lamont

44 www.katielear.com/child-therapy-blog/2020/2/7/racial-mirrors-windows-multicultural-books

45 mediaschool.indiana.edu/news-events/news/item.html?n=weaver-article-racial-bias-in-film-preference-can-be-overcome

46 www.statista.com/statistics/1095814/foreign-language-film-preferences-us-by-ethnicity/

47 www.nytimes.com/2020/05/01/your-money/philanthropy-race.html

48 www.aaas.org/news/technologys-built-machine-bias-reflects-racism-scholar-says

49 www.aclu.org/news/privacy-technology/how-is-face-recognition-surveillance-technology-racist/

If you're interested in finding out more about our books, find us on Facebook at Summersdale Publishers and follow us on Twitter at @Summersdale and on Instagram at @SummersdalePublishers.

www.summersdale.com